California Legislative Scorecard: 2015 Session

Copyright © 2016 | California Civil Liberties Advocacy, Inc.

California Civil Liberties Advocacy
1242 Bridge St. #65
Yuba City, CA 95991
http://www.CaliforniaCivilLiberties.org/

Printed in the United States of America

About the CCLA

The California Civil Liberties Advocacy (CCLA) is a nonpartisan, statewide, 501(c)(4) nonprofit public benefit organization, which advocates for California state laws and policies that accentuate the personal rights and liberties of individuals residing within the state.

The CCLA began in 2013 with an unincorporated group of citizens who had become disillusioned with the status quo in California and the United States as a whole. With a prison population higher than any other country in the world, dishonest law enforcement tactics, soaring police brutality, constant government intrusion into private affairs, and et cetera, the time was at hand for common citizens to band together in order to "petition their government for a redress of grievances."

The CCLA engages directly with the California State Legislature and administrative agencies, endeavoring to inform the public on important policies, and enable them to hold accountable the lawmakers behind those policies by engaging in grassroots advocacy and direct lobbying.

No matter where you look in society, by far the gravest threat to liberty is apathy. Many do not realize that programs like the NSA's bulk data collection is only the tip of the iceberg. Local law enforcement is using advanced technology to spy on people in their community just as the NSA, CIA, or FBI do. Education and awareness is crucial to combatting these problems. And many people often overlook the fact that, besides the famous checks and balances between the executive, legislative, and judicial branches, there is one more powerful check on all three — we the people! The people can exercise this power by voting, by writing to elected representatives, and by speaking out in the press.

Even before this land was discovered by Europeans in 1542, California existed as dream — an enchanted, Edenic land that was romanticized in Garci Rodríguez de Montalvo's novel, "Las Sergas de Esplandian." Since then, California has been captured in the minds of people all over the world as a land of innovation, enterprise, democracy, and progressivism.

While California has not always lived up to its reputation, the state often serves as a model for the federal and other state governments when implementing public policy. In this way, we believe California can still be exceptional, as the economic, social, and political final frontier.

The CCLA believes in the idea of California's exceptionalism and seek to augment the progressive ideals and policies of some of California's past leaders, such as Hiram Johnson and Earl Warren. The CCLA also believes in the United States Constitution and the Bill of Rights as the fundamental law by which to ensure the rights of individuals in the state and abroad. It is noteworthy that California's constitution is even more progressive than the United Sates Constitution, offering greater protections and acknowledging a broader spectrum of what are to be considered "inalienable rights." Article I, section 1 states that "All people are by nature free and independent and have inalienable rights. Among these are enjoying and defending life and liberty, acquiring, possessing, and protecting property, and pursuing and obtaining safety, happiness, and privacy." Section 8 of California's constitution explicitly prohibits discrimination "because of sex, race, creed, color, or national or ethnic origin."

The CCLA believes that all people are created equal and are endowed with inalienable rights, including the enjoyment and defense of life, liberty, and property and aggressively advocates for legislation, regulations, and public policies that uphold and augment these rights.

About the Scorecard

Many special interest and grassroots advocacy groups on the federal and state levels maintain a scorecard of their lawmakers. Legislative scorecards serve several purposes. For one thing, a scorecard offers abundant insight into the voting propensities of each individual lawmaker, which can help to inform the public who can, in turn, hold their representatives accountable by contacting their office and voting either for or against them in the upcoming election.

Scorecards also serve as a check on lawmakers, letting them know that their actions are being scrutinized, which collaterally encourages them to consider the issues more carefully. Every lawmaker in the California legislature was provided a copy of the scorecard and a cover letter informing them of their grade. In this case, lawmakers are put on notice that their values and attitudes toward civil liberties may not be aligned with the best interests of the general population, who typically take such rights for granted.

Additionally, scorecards allow individuals and advocates to ascertain where their legislature stands as a whole. Like Congress, California utilizes a bi-cameral legislature, meaning that it is comprised of two chambers — the Assembly, with 80 members, and the Senate, with 40 senators. Interestingly, scorecards offer a measure of transparency, allowing the voting public to see how political views and party affiliations affect a lawmaker's choices. As can be seen from this year's scorecard, sometimes party affiliations have nothing to do with a lawmaker's voting outcomes.

The CCLA's Grading System

Lawmakers are typically graded based on their voting outcomes on a sample of bills related to a group's cause. In this case, California's legislators were graded based on a sample of eleven bills that would have impacted civil liberties for individuals in California either negatively or positively.

For a bill that positively impacted civil liberties, a legislator was awarded one point if they voted in favor of that bill, or docked one point if they voted against it. For a bill that negatively impacted civil liberties, a legislator was docked one point if they voted in favor of it, or awarded one point if they voted against it. Bills enclosed in parentheses indicates a negative impact on civil liberties.

Legislators who abstained from voting lost a half-point, rather than being excluded in the final tally. This is because some lawmakers exhibit a pattern of abstaining from voting on bills that may appear to be controversial. For instance, one bill that was very controversial was AB 953, which expanded the definitions of racial profiling and required law enforcement to keep detailed records of every stop. Lobbyists for law enforcement organizations worked very hard to prevent the passage of AB 953 and many legislators abstained from voting. The bill passed nonetheless, but the CCLA took note of those who were apparently hesitant to take a stand one way or another. It is true that some legislators may not have been able to vote due to various reasonable circumstances. However, those who exhibit a tendency to abstain for fear of public rejection must also be put on notice that their refusal to make a choice is also being scrutinized. And it stands to reason that if these issues were as important to those legislators who could not be present to vote for a legitimate reason, then they would have been there to make sure their vote was counted. Their absence signals to civil liberties advocates that the issue was not important enough for them to adjust their schedule to make those bills priority.

Example:

Name	Party	AB 69	AB 71	AB 953	AB 929	SB 34	SB 142	SB 411	SB 178	SB 741	(SB 249)	SB 443	Total	%	Grade
Chávez, Rocky J.	Rep	Y	Y	N	Y	Y	N	Y	nv	Y	(Y)	N	6.5/11	59%	F

Assemblymember Rocky Chávez voted "Yes" on six bills that have a positive impact on civil liberties, "No" on three bills that have a positive impact, "Yes" on one bill that has a negative impact, and abstained on one bill that has a positive impact. So out of a possible 11 total points,

Assemblymember Chávez's score was calculated as follows:

$$(11 - 4.5) / 11 = 0.59 \times 100 = 59\%$$

Grading Scale:

95-100% = A +	70-74% = C –
90-94% = A –	65-69% = D +
85-89% = B +	60-64% = D –
80-84% = B –	≤ 59% = F
75-79% = C +	

While some may interpret the voting propensities of a legislator who received an "F" to be "moderate," having potentially voted in favor of civil liberties issues more than half of the time, such an interpretation is only nominal at best and inaccurate to say the least. Over a thousand bills are introduced between the two chambers of California's legislature, many of which either directly or indirectly affect civil liberties, and this sample only represents a small portion. And the CCLA has determined that these bills represent good policies that favor the peoples' best interests. Drawing a line down the center and concluding that a legislator is statistically "moderate" is asinine. After all, if a lawmaker can only reliably be expected to vote in favor of civil liberties—the interests of the people they purport to represent—about fifty to sixty percent of the time, then it is impossible to predict how they will vote on very serious issues, such as individual privacy, due process, or even victims' claims and compensation.

It is noteworthy that out of California's 120 legislators, only one received an A+ — Assemblymember Marc Levine (D) from the 10th Assembly District. Mr. Levine obtained a perfect score, voting in the best interests of the people on 100% of the bills in our sample. Also noteworthy is that the lowest scoring lawmaker was Assemblymember Shannon Grove (R) from the 34th Assembly District, who voted in favor of civil liberties on less than 50% of the bills in our sample, at 45%.

As a whole, the California State Senate scored an average of 79%, signaling that it is <u>slightly</u> more progressive on civil liberties issue than the

Assembly, which scored 77%. The average score of both chambers combined was 79%, which would equal a C+, meaning that California's legislature is somewhat moderate when considered *in toto.*

The Bill Sample

The eleven bills sampled for this scorecard represent a range of issues, including individual privacy, due process, freedom of speech, law enforcement accountability, suspect profiling, and civil asset forfeiture. A more detailed description of each bill is provided below:

Assembly Bill 69
(Freddie Rodriguez-D)

Signed into law by Governor Brown and effective January 1, 2016, AB 69 would require law enforcement agencies to consider best practices when establishing polices regarding the download and storage of body camera footage. Body cameras have been shown to increase law enforcement accountability and transparency. AB 69 is the first legislation in the state to establish statewide standards for the use of body cameras by police officers. Lawmakers received a positive score if they voted in favor of this bill.

Assembly Bill 71
(Freddie Rodriguez-D)

Signed into law by Governor Brown and effective January 1, 2017, AB 71 will require law enforcement agencies to submit an annual report to the Department of Justice regarding officers involved in shootings or incidents of serious bodily injury. The report will contain demographic and statistical data of cases in which individuals or officers are injured or killed. The Department of Justice will be required to include in its annual crime report a summary of the incident reports from each jurisdiction. Making all of this information available in public reports will work to increase law enforcement accountability and enhance transparency. Lawmakers received a positive score if they voted in favor of this bill.

Assembly Bill 953
(Shirley Weber-D)

Signed into law by Governor Brown and effective January 1, 2016, AB 953 modifies the definition of "racial profiling" to "racial or identity profiling" and prohibits law enforcement from profiling suspects based upon perceived race, color, ethnicity, national origin, religion, gender identity, sexual orientation, or mental or physical disabilities. As of July 1, 2016, the Attorney General must establish the Racial and Identity Profiling Advisory Board (RIPA) to investigate state and local law enforcement policies and practices, to publish annual reports, and hold public meetings. Beginning March 1, 2018, local agencies will be required to report to the Attorney General's office data on all stops, including the reason for the stop, the result, whether an arrest was made and the offense charged, and the perceived race or ethnicity, gender, and approximate age of the person stopped. Lawmakers received a positive score if they voted in favor of this bill.

Assembly Bill 929
(Ed Chau-D)

Signed into law by Governor Brown and effective January 1, 2016, AB 929 defines "pen register" as a device or process that records or decodes dialing, routing, addressing, or signaling information from a device or facility that transmits a wire or electronic communication, not including the contents of the communication. AB 929 defines "trap and trace" devices as a device or process that captures incoming electronic or other impulses that reveal the originating number or other dialing, routing, address, or signaling information, not including the contents of a communication. AB 929 also defines the type of offenses for which a court order to install such devices may be granted and prohibits law enforcement from installing or using pen register or trap and trace devices absent a court order based on probable cause, and unless relevant to an ongoing criminal investigation. Violating this requirement could result in a $2,500 fine, up to one year in a county jail, and/or up to three years in prison. Lawmakers received a positive score if they voted in favor of this bill.

Senate Bill 34
(Jerry Hill-D)

Signed into law by Governor Brown and effective January 1, 2016, SB 34 establishes regulations on the privacy and usage of automatic license plate recognition (ALPR) data and expands the meaning of "personal information" to include information or data collected through the use or operation of an ALPR system. As a companion bill to SB 178, SB 34 provides a framework that will establish basic policies designed to enhance privacy, and procedural requirements outlining the security, usage, and storage of ALPR data. SB 34 also sets up chain of custody procedures that extend accountability and provides civil remedies for anyone harmed by a person who knowingly violates those requirements. SB 34 will also prohibit public agencies from selling or sharing ALPR data, except to other public agencies specified within the bill. Lawmakers received a positive score if they voted in favor of this bill.

Senate Bill 142
(Hannah-Beth Jackson-D)

Passed by both the Assembly and the Senate in August of 2015, Senate Bill 142 was vetoed by Governor Brown on September 9th, 2015 and would have established a no-fly zone for unmanned aircraft and unmanned aircraft systems (also known as "drones"), prohibiting flight over private property below 350 feet without the consent of the owner. A drone operator flying below 350 feet over private property would have been liable for trespass. The bill established a cause of action that would have allowed harmed property owners to collect damages from the offending operator. Lawmakers received a positive score if they voted in favor of this bill.

Senate Bill 411
(Ricardo Lara-D)

Signed into law by Governor Brown and effective January 1, 2016, Senate Bill 411 effectively bars law enforcement from arresting members of the public for exercising their First Amendment right to take photographs or make audio or video recordings of police and their interactions with the public, which increase transparency and accountability in police interactions with the public. Lawmakers received a positive score if they voted in favor of this bill.

Senate Bill 178
(Mark Leno-D)

Signed into law by Governor Brown and effective January 1, 2016, the California Electronic Communications Privacy Act ("CalECPA") is an update to the federal Electronic Communications Privacy Act of 1986. SB 178 will prevent law enforcement and other government entities from accessing private data by compelling production from service providers, third parties, or by physically or electronically interacting with an electronic device. Law enforcement and government entities will now be required to seek a warrant, wiretap order, or subpoena to gain access to such data. Alternatively, law enforcement may gain access to private data with the consent of the device's owner. Lawmakers received a positive score if they voted in favor of this bill.

Senate Bill 741
(Jerry Hill-D)

Signed into law by Governor Brown and effective January 1, 2016, SB 741 establishes regulations on the privacy and usage of cellphone data acquired by use of cellular communications intercept devices (commonly known as "Stingray"), which are capable of mimicking cellphone towers. As a companion bill to SB 178, SB 741 provides a framework that will establish basic policies designed to enhance privacy, and procedural requirements outlining the security, usage, and storage of ALPR data. These policies are required to be conspicuously posted on the agency's website. Local agencies will also be prohibited (except for county sheriff departments) from implementing cellular intercept devices unless approved by a resolution or ordinance at a regularly scheduled public meetings. SB 741 also sets up chain of custody procedures that extend accountability and provides civil remedies for anyone harmed by a person who knowingly violates those requirements. Lawmakers received a positive score if they voted in favor of this bill.

Senate Bill 249
(Hueso-D)

Passed by the Assembly and the Senate on September 11th and subsequently vetoed by Governor Brown on October 9th, 2015, Senate Bill 249 would have authorized the DMV to work with the federal government to issue "enhanced driver's licenses" that contain an RFID chip that could be scanned by border patrol to make it easier for travelers when crossing the U.S.-Mexico border. These enhanced driver's licenses would have posed a threat to individual privacy as the RFID chips could be read remotely, for instance, 30 feet away or more, and without the knowledge or consent of the license holder. The RFID chips would contain a unique number identifying the individual, which could be searched in a database by law enforcement and used to profile suspects absent a reasonable suspicion or probable cause. Lawmakers received a negative score if they voted in favor of this bill.

Senate Bill 443
(Holly Mitchell-D)

Passed in the Senate on June 3rd 38 to 1 in favor, but failed passage in the Assembly 24 to 44 on September 9th, 2015, Senate Bill 443 would have substantially reformed the law enforcement practice of civil asset forfeiture in California. State law provides fairly strict protections for citizens subject to asset forfeiture, however a loophole in federal law allows state and local law enforcement agencies to work with the federal government, thereby circumventing state law, and allowing law such agencies to receive 80% of the proceeds. SB 443 would have made it illegal for state and local law enforcement agencies to participate in these federal programs, allocated some of the proceeds equally to local prosecutors and public defenders, and allowed parties to recover reasonable attorneys' fees when prevailing against the government in such forfeiture actions. Lawmakers received a positive score if they voted in favor of this bill.

For more information on these and other bills, visit the California Legislative Information website at http://leginfo.legislature.ca.gov/

2015 Legislative Scorecard

Below are the scores for all 120 members of the California State Legislature, plus Governor Jerry Brown. The various grades have been color-coded for easy identification.

Y = Yea   N = Noe   nv = No Vote   S = Signed   V = Veto   P = Passed without governor's signature

■ = A   ■ = B   ■ = C   ■ = D   ■ = F   Rep = Republican   Dem = Democrat

Name	Party	AB 69	AB 71	AB 953	AB 929	SB 34	SB 142	SB 411	SB 178	SB 741	(SB 249)	SB 443	Total	%	Grade
Office of the Governor															
Jerry Brown	Dem	S	S	S	S	S	V	S	S	S	V	N/A	9/10	90%	A
State Assembly															
Achadjian, Katcho	Rep	Y	Y	N	Y	Y	Y	Y	Y	Y	(Y)	N	8/11	73%	C -
Alejo, Luis A.	Dem	Y	Y	Y	Y	Y	Y	Y	nv	Y	(Y)	N	8.5/11	77%	C +
Allen, Travis	Rep	Y	Y	N	Y	Y	N	Y	Y	Y	(Y)	N	7/11	64%	D -
Atkins, Toni G.	Dem	Y	Y	Y	Y	Y	Y	Y	Y	Y	(Y)	Y	10/11	91%	A -
Baker, Catharine B.	Rep	Y	Y	N	Y	Y	Y	Y	N	Y	(Y)	N	7/11	64%	D -
Bigelow, Frank	Rep	Y	Y	N	Y	Y	nv	Y	Y	Y	(Y)	N	7.5/11	68%	D +
Bloom, Richard	Dem	Y	Y	Y	Y	Y	Y	Y	Y	Y	(Y)	Y	10/11	91%	A -
Bonilla, Susan A.	Dem	Y	Y	Y	Y	Y	Y	Y	Y	Y	(Y)	nv	9.5/11	86%	B +
Bonta, Rob	Dem	Y	Y	Y	Y	Y	nv	Y	Y	Y	(Y)	Y	9.5/11	86%	B +
Brough, William P.	Rep	Y	Y	N	Y	Y	Y	N	N	Y	(nv)	Y	7.5/11	68%	D +
Brown, Cheryl R.	Dem	Y	Y	Y	Y	Y	Y	Y	Y	Y	(Y)	nv	9.5/11	86%	B +
Burke, Autumn R.	Dem	Y	Y	Y	Y	Y	Y	Y	Y	Y	(Y)	Y	10/11	91%	A -
Calderon, Ian C.	Dem	Y	Y	Y	Y	Y	Y	Y	nv	Y	(Y)	N	8.5/11	77%	C +
Campos, Nora	Dem	Y	Y	Y	Y	Y	Y	Y	Y	Y	(Y)	nv	9.5/11	86%	B +
Chang, Ling Ling	Rep	Y	Y	N	Y	Y	nv	Y	Y	Y	(Y)	N	7.5/11	68%	D +
Chau, Ed	Dem	Y	Y	Y	Y	Y	Y	Y	Y	Y	(Y)	nv	9.5/11	86%	B +
Chávez, Rocky J.	Rep	Y	Y	N	Y	Y	N	Y	nv	Y	(Y)	N	6.5/11	59%	F
Chiu, David	Dem	Y	Y	Y	Y	Y	Y	Y	Y	Y	(Y)	Y	10/11	91%	A -
Chu, Kansen	Dem	Y	Y	Y	Y	Y	Y	Y	Y	Y	(Y)	N	9/11	81%	B -
Cooley, Ken	Dem	Y	Y	Y	Y	Y	Y	Y	Y	Y	(Y)	N	9/11	81%	B -
Cooper, Jim	Dem	Y	Y	nv	Y	Y	Y	Y	N	Y	(Y)	N	7.5/11	68%	D +

Name	Party	AB 69	AB 71	AB 953	AB 929	SB 34	SB 142	SB 411	SB 178	SB 741	(SB 249)	SB 443	Total	%	Grade
Dababneh, Matthew	Dem	Y	Y	Y	Y	Y	Y	Y	Y	Y	(Y)	Y	10/11	91%	A -
Dahle, Brian	Rep	Y	Y	N	Y	Y	Y	Y	N	Y	(nv)	N	8.5/11	77%	C +
Daly, Tom	Dem	Y	Y	Y	Y	Y	nv	Y	nv	Y	(Y)	N	8/11	73%	C -
Dodd, Bill	Dem	Y	Y	Y	Y	Y	Y	Y	Y	Y	(Y)	N	9/11	81%	B -
Eggman, Susan Talamantes	Dem	Y	Y	Y	Y	Y	Y	Y	Y	Y	(Y)	nv	9.5/11	86%	B +
Frazier, Jim	Dem	Y	Y	nv	Y	Y	nv	Y	N	Y	(Y)	N	7/11	64%	D -
Gaines, Beth B.	Rep	Y	Y	N	Y	nv	Y	N	nv	nv	(Y)	N	5.5/11	50%	F
Gallagher, James	Rep	Y	Y	N	Y	nv	Y	nv	nv	Y	(Y)	N	6.5/11	59%	F
Garcia, Cristina	Dem	Y	Y	Y	Y	Y	Y	Y	Y	Y	(Y)	Y	10/11	91%	A -
Garcia, Eduardo	Dem	Y	Y	Y	Y	Y	Y	Y	Y	Y	(Y)	N	9/11	81%	B -
Gatto, Mike	Dem	Y	Y	N	Y	Y	Y	Y	Y	Y	(N)	N	9/11	81%	B -
Gipson, Mike A.	Dem	Y	Y	Y	Y	Y	N	Y	nv	Y	(Y)	nv	8/11	73%	C -
Gomez, Jimmy	Dem	Y	Y	Y	Y	Y	Y	Y	Y	Y	(Y)	nv	9.5/11	86%	B +
Gonzalez, Lorena S.	Dem	Y	Y	Y	Y	Y	Y	Y	Y	Y	(Y)	nv	9.5/11	86%	B +
Gordon, Richard S.	Dem	Y	Y	Y	Y	Y	nv	Y	Y	Y	(Y)	N	9.5/11	86%	B +
Gray, Adam C.	Dem	Y	Y	N	Y	Y	nv	Y	N	Y	(Y)	N	7.5/11	68%	D +
Grove, Shannon L.	Rep	Y	Y	N	nv	N	N	nv	Y	Y	(Y)	N	5/11	45%	F
Hadley, David	Rep	Y	Y	N	Y	Y	N	Y	Y	Y	(Y)	Y	8/11	73%	C -
Harper, Matthew	Rep	nv	Y	N	Y	Y	Y	nv	Y	Y	(nv)	Y	8.5/11	77%	C +
Hernández, Roger	Dem	Y	Y	Y	Y	Y	Y	Y	Y	Y	(Y)	N	9/11	81%	B -
Holden, Chris R.	Dem	Y	Y	Y	Y	Y	Y	Y	Y	Y	(Y)	Y	10/11	91%	A -
Irwin, Jacqui	Dem	Y	Y	nv	Y	Y	Y	Y	N	Y	(Y)	N	7.5/11	68%	D +
Jones, Brian W.	Rep	Y	Y	N	Y	N	N	Y	Y	Y	(Y)	N	6/11	55%	F
Jones-Sawyer, Sr., Reginald B.	Dem	Y	Y	Y	Y	Y	Y	Y	Y	Y	(Y)	Y	10/11	91%	A -
Kim, Young O.	Rep	Y	Y	N	Y	Y	Y	Y	nv	Y	(Y)	N	7.5/11	68%	D +
Lackey, Tom	Rep	Y	nv	N	Y	Y	Y	Y	Y	Y	(Y)	N	7.5/11	68%	D +
Levine, Marc	Dem	Y	Y	Y	Y	Y	Y	Y	Y	Y	(N)	Y	11/11	100%	A +
Linder, Eric	Rep	Y	Y	N	Y	Y	nv	Y	N	Y	(Y)	N	6.5/11	59%	F
López, Patty	Dem	Y	Y	Y	Y	Y	Y	Y	Y	Y	(Y)	N	10/11	91%	A -
Low, Evan	Dem	Y	Y	Y	Y	Y	Y	Y	Y	Y	(Y)	N	9/11	81%	B -
Maienschein, Brian	Rep	Y	Y	N	Y	Y	Y	Y	Y	Y	(Y)	N	9/11	81%	B -
Mathis, Devon J.	Rep	Y	Y	N	Y	N	N	Y	Y	Y	(Y)	N	6/11	55%	F
Mayes, Chad	Rep	Y	Y	N	Y	Y	Y	Y	Y	Y	(Y)	N	8/11	73%	C -
McCarty, Kevin	Dem	Y	Y	Y	Y	Y	Y	Y	Y	Y	(Y)	Y	10/11	91%	A -

Name	Party	AB 69	AB 71	AB 953	AB 929	SB 34	SB 142	SB 411	SB 178	SB 741	(SB 249)	SB 443	Total	%	Grade
Medina, Jose	Dem	Y	Y	Y	Y	Y	N	Y	N	Y	(Y)	N	7/11	64%	D -
Melendez, Melissa A.	Rep	Y	Y	N	Y	nv	Y	Y	Y	Y	(Y)	N	7.5/11	68%	D +
Mullin, Kevin	Dem	Y	Y	Y	Y	Y	N	Y	Y	Y	(Y)	nv	8.5/11	77%	C +
Nazarian, Adrin	Dem	Y	Y	Y	Y	Y	Y	Y	Y	Y	(Y)	nv	9.5/11	86%	B +
Obernolte, Jay	Rep	Y	Y	N	Y	N	N	Y	Y	Y	(Y)	nv	6.5/11	59%	F
O'Donnell, Patrick	Dem	Y	Y	nv	Y	Y	Y	Y	nv	Y	(Y)	N	8/11	73%	C -
Olsen, Kristin	Rep	Y	Y	N	Y	Y	nv	nv	Y	Y	(Y)	N	7/11	64%	D -
Patterson, Jim	Rep	Y	Y	N	Y	nv	Y	Y	Y	Y	(Y)	N	7.5/11	68%	D +
Perea, Henry T.	Dem	Y	Y	nv	Y	Y	N	Y	N	Y	(Y)	N	6.5/11	59%	F
Quirk, Bill	Dem	Y	Y	Y	Y	Y	nv	Y	Y	Y	(Y)	Y	9.5/11	86%	B +
Rendon, Anthony	Dem	Y	Y	Y	Y	Y	Y	Y	Y	Y	(Y)	Y	10/11	91%	A -
Ridley-Thomas, Sebastian	Dem	Y	Y	Y	Y	Y	Y	Y	N	Y	(Y)	nv	8.5/11	77%	C +
Rodriguez, Freddie	Dem	Y	Y	nv	Y	Y	Y	Y	Y	Y	(Y)	N	9.5/11	86%	B +
Salas, Jr., Rudy	Dem	Y	Y	Y	Y	Y	Y	Y	nv	Y	(Y)	N	8.5/11	77%	C +
Santiago, Miguel	Dem	Y	Y	Y	Y	Y	Y	Y	Y	Y	(Y)	Y	10/11	91%	A -
Steinorth, Marc	Rep	Y	Y	N	Y	Y	Y	Y	Y	Y	(Y)	N	8/11	73%	C -
Stone, Mark	Dem	Y	Y	Y	Y	Y	Y	Y	Y	Y	(Y)	Y	10/11	91%	A -
Thurmond, Tony	Dem	Y	Y	Y	Y	Y	Y	Y	Y	Y	(Y)	Y	10/11	91%	A -
Ting, Philip Y.	Dem	Y	Y	Y	Y	Y	N	Y	Y	Y	(Y)	Y	10/11	91%	A -
Wagner, Donald P.	Rep	Y	Y	N	Y	N	N	Y	Y	Y	(Y)	N	6/11	55%	F
Waldron, Marie	Rep	Y	Y	N	Y	Y	nv	Y	N	Y	(nv)	N	8/11	73%	C -
Weber, Shirley N.	Dem	Y	Y	Y	Y	Y	Y	Y	Y	Y	(Y)	Y	10/11	91%	A -
Wilk, Scott	Rep	Y	Y	N	Y	Y	Y	Y	Y	Y	(Y)	N	8/11	73%	C -
Williams, Das	Dem	Y	Y	nv	Y	Y	Y	Y	N	Y	(nv)	N	8/11	73%	C -
Wood, Jim	Dem	Y	Y	Y	Y	Y	Y	Y	Y	Y	(Y)	N	9/11	81%	B -
State Senate															
Allen, Benjamin	Dem	Y	Y	Y	Y	Y	Y	Y	Y	Y	(Y)	Y	10/11	91%	A -
Anderson, Joel	Rep	Y	Y	N	Y	N	N	N	Y	Y	(Y)	Y	6/11	55%	F
Bates, Patricia C.	Rep	Y	Y	N	Y	N	nv	N	Y	Y	(Y)	Y	6.5/11	59%	F
Beall, Jim	Dem	Y	Y	Y	Y	nv	Y	Y	Y	Y	(Y)	Y	9.5/11	86%	B +
Berryhill, Tom	Rep	Y	Y	N	Y	N	N	N	Y	Y	(Y)	Y	7/11	64%	D -
Block, Marty	Dem	Y	Y	Y	Y	Y	nv	Y	Y	Y	(Y)	Y	9.5/11	86%	B +
Canella, Anthony	Rep	Y	Y	N	Y	Y	N	Y	Y	Y	(Y)	Y	8/11	73%	C -
de León, Kevin	Dem	Y	Y	Y	Y	Y	Y	Y	Y	Y	(Y)	Y	10/11	91%	A -

Name	Party	AB 69	AB 71	AB 953	AB 929	SB 34	SB 142	SB 411	SB 178	SB 741	(SB 249)	SB 443	Total	%	Grade
Fuller, Jean	Rep	Y	Y	N	Y	N	N	Y	Y	Y	(Y)	Y	7/11	64%	D -
Gaines, Ted	Rep	Y	Y	N	Y	N	Y	nv	Y	Y	(Y)	Y	7.5/11	68%	D +
Galgiani, Cathleen	Dem	Y	Y	nv	Y	Y	N	Y	N	Y	(Y)	Y	7.5/11	68%	D +
Glazer, Steven M.	Dem	Y	Y	Y	Y	Y	N	Y	Y	Y	(Y)	Y	9/11	81%	B -
Hall III, Isidore	Dem	Y	Y	Y	Y	Y	nv	Y	nv	Y	(Y)	Y	9/11	81%	B -
Hancock, Loni	Dem	Y	Y	Y	Y	Y	Y	Y	Y	Y	(Y)	Y	10/11	91%	A -
Hernandez, Ed	Dem	Y	Y	Y	Y	Y	nv	Y	Y	Y	(Y)	Y	9.5/11	86%	B +
Hertzberg, Robert M.	Dem	Y	Y	Y	Y	Y	Y	Y	Y	Y	(Y)	Y	10/11	91%	A -
Hill, Jerry	Dem	Y	Y	Y	Y	Y	N	Y	Y	Y	(Y)	Y	9/11	81%	B -
Hueso, Ben	Dem	Y	Y	Y	Y	Y	Y	Y	Y	Y	(Y)	Y	10/11	91%	A -
Huff, Bob	Rep	Y	Y	N	Y	N	N	Y	Y	Y	(Y)	Y	7/11	64%	D -
Jackson, Hannah-Beth	Dem	Y	Y	Y	Y	nv	Y	Y	Y	Y	(Y)	Y	9.5/11	86%	B +
Lara, Ricardo	Dem	Y	Y	Y	Y	Y	Y	Y	Y	Y	(Y)	Y	10/11	91%	A -
Leno, Mark	Dem	Y	Y	Y	Y	Y	Y	Y	Y	Y	(Y)	Y	10/11	91%	A -
Leyva, Connie M.	Dem	Y	Y	Y	Y	Y	Y	Y	Y	Y	(Y)	N	10/11	91%	A -
Liu, Carol	Dem	Y	Y	Y	Y	Y	Y	nv	Y	Y	(Y)	Y	9.5/11	86%	B +
McGuire, Mike	Dem	Y	Y	Y	Y	Y	Y	Y	Y	Y	(Y)	Y	10/11	91%	A -
Mendoza, Tony	Dem	Y	Y	Y	Y	Y	Y	Y	Y	Y	(Y)	Y	10/11	91%	A -
Mitchell, Holly J.	Dem	Y	Y	Y	Y	Y	Y	Y	Y	Y	(Y)	Y	10/11	91%	A -
Monning, Bill	Dem	Y	Y	Y	Y	Y	Y	Y	Y	Y	(Y)	Y	10/11	91%	A -
Moorlach, John M. W.	Rep	Y	Y	Y	Y	N	nv	Y	Y	Y	(nv)	Y	9/11	81%	B -
Morell, Mike	Rep	Y	Y	N	Y	N	N	N	Y	Y	(N)	Y	7/11	64%	D-
Nguyen, Janet	Rep	Y	Y	N	Y	N	nv	Y	N	Y	(Y)	Y	6.5/11	59%	F
Nielsen, Jim	Rep	Y	Y	N	Y	nv	nv	nv	Y	Y	(Y)	nv	7/11	64%	D -
Pan, Richard	Dem	Y	Y	Y	Y	Y	Y	Y	Y	Y	(Y)	Y	10/11	91%	A -
Pavley, Fran	Dem	Y	Y	Y	Y	Y	Y	nv	Y	Y	(Y)	Y	9.5/11	86%	B +
Roth, Richard D.	Dem	Y	Y	Y	Y	Y	Y	Y	Y	Y	(Y)	Y	10/11	91%	A -
Runner, Sharon	Rep	Y	Y	N	nv	N	N	nv	nv	Y	(Y)	Y	5.5/11	50%	F
Stone, Jeff	Rep	Y	Y	N	Y	nv	N	Y	N	Y	(Y)	Y	6.5/11	59%	F
Vidak, Andy	Rep	Y	Y	N	Y	N	N	Y	N	Y	(Y)	Y	6/11	55%	F
Wieckowski, Bob	Dem	Y	Y	Y	Y	Y	Y	Y	Y	Y	(Y)	Y	10/11	91%	A -
Wolk, Lois	Dem	Y	Y	Y	Y	Y	Y	Y	Y	Y	(Y)	Y	10/11	91%	A -

Assemblymembers by District

Dist.	Assemblymember	Party
1	Brian Dahle	Rep
2	Jim Wood	Dem
3	James Gallagher	Rep
4	Bill Dodd	Dem
5	Frank Bigelow	Rep
6	Beth Gaines	Rep
7	Kevin McCarty	Dem
8	Ken Cooley	Dem
9	Jim Cooper	Dem
10	Marc Levine	Dem
11	Jim Frazier	Dem
12	Kristin Olsen	Rep
13	Susan Talamantes Eggman	Dem
14	Susan Bonilla	Dem
15	Tony Thurmond	Dem
16	Catharine Baker	Rep
17	David Chiu	Dem
18	Rob Bonta	Dem
19	Phil Ting	Dem
20	Bill Quirk	Dem
21	Adam Gray	Dem
22	Kevin Mullin	Dem
23	Jim Patterson	Rep
24	Rich Gordon	Dem
25	Kansen Chu	Dem
26	Devon Mathis	Rep
27	Nora Campos	Dem
28	Evan Low	Dem
29	Mark Stone	Dem
30	Luis Alejo	Dem
31	Vacant	
32	Rudy Salas	Dem
33	Jay Obernolte	Rep
34	Shannon Grove	Rep
35	K.H. Achadjian	Rep
36	Tom Lackey	Rep
37	Das Williams	Dem
38	Scott Wilk	Rep
39	Patty Lopez	Dem
40	Marc Steinorth	Rep
41	Chris Holden	Dem
42	Chad Mayes	Rep
43	Mike Gatto	Dem
44	Jacqui Irwin	Dem
45	Matt Dababneh	Dem
46	Adrin Nazarian	Dem
47	Cheryl Brown	Dem
48	Roger Hernandez	Dem
49	Edwin Chau	Dem
50	Richard Bloom	Dem
51	Jimmy Gomez	Dem
52	Freddie Rodriguez	Dem
53	Miguel Santiago	Dem
54	Sebastian Ridley-Thomas	Dem
55	Ling-Ling Chang	Rep
56	Eduardo Garcia	Dem
57	Ian Charles Calderon	Dem
58	Cristina Garcia	Dem
59	Reginald Jones-Sawyer	Dem
60	Eric Linder	Rep
61	Jose Medina	Dem
62	Autumn Burke	Dem
63	Anthony Rendon	Dem
64	Mike Gipson	Dem
65	Young Kim	Rep
66	David Hadley	Rep
67	Melissa Melendez	Rep
68	Donald P. Wagner	Rep
69	Tom Daly	Dem
70	Patrick O'Donnell	Dem
71	Brian Jones	Rep
72	Travis Allen	Rep
73	William Brough	Rep
74	Matthew Harper	Rep
75	Marie Waldron	Rep
76	Rocky Chavez	Rep
77	Brian Maienschein	Rep
78	Toni Atkins	Dem
79	Shirley Weber	Dem
80	Lorena Gonzalez	Dem

State Assembly District Map

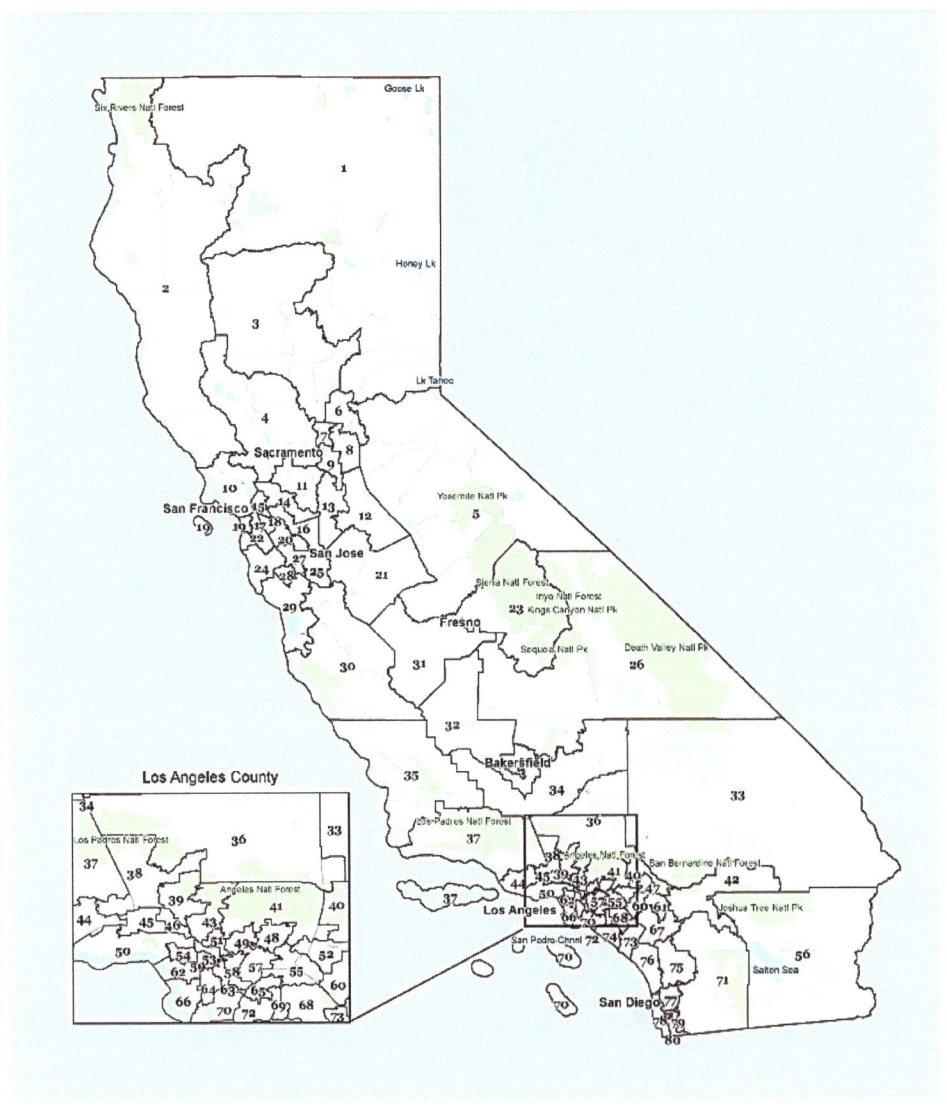

Senators by District

Dist.	Assemblymember	Party
1	Ted Gaines	Rep
2	Mike McGuire	Dem
3	Lois Wolk	Dem
4	Jim Nielsen	Rep
5	Cathleen Galgiani	Dem
6	Richard Pan	Dem
7	Steve Glazer	Dem
8	Tom Berryhill	Rep
9	Loni Hancock	Dem
10	Bob Wieckowski	Dem
11	Mark Leno	Dem
12	Anthony Cannella	Rep
13	Gerald Hill	Dem
14	Andy Vidak	Rep
15	James Beall Jr.	Dem
16	Jean Fuller	Rep
17	Bill Monning	Dem
18	Robert Hertzberg	Dem
19	Hannah-Beth Jackson	Dem
20	Connie M. Leyva	Dem
21	Sharon Runner	Rep
22	Edward Hernandez	Dem
23	Mike Morrell	Rep
24	Kevin de León	Dem
25	Carol Liu	Dem
26	Ben Allen	Dem
27	Fran Pavley	Dem
28	Jeff Stone	Rep
29	Bob Huff	Rep
30	Holly Mitchell	Dem
31	Richard Roth	Dem
32	Tony Mendoza	Dem
33	Ricardo Lara	Dem
34	Janet Nguyen	Rep
35	Isadore Hall, III	Dem
36	Patricia C. Bates	Rep
37	John Moorlach	Rep
38	Joel Anderson	Rep
39	Martin Block	Dem
40	Ben Hueso	Dem

State Senate District Map

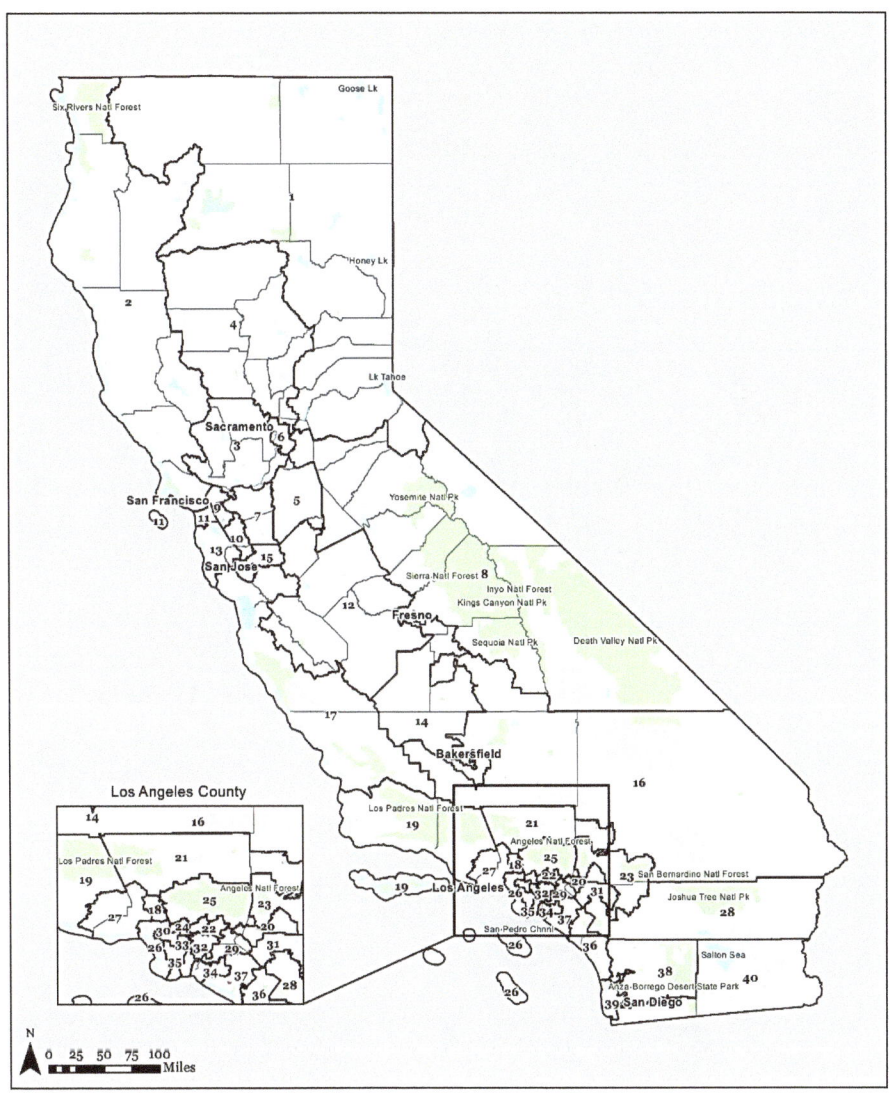

Contact Us

To get in touch with the CCLA, call or write to us at:

California Civil Liberties Advocacy
1242 Bridge St. #65
Yuba City, CA 95991

(916) 741-2560

ccla@caliberty.net

For more information on the California Civil Liberties Advocacy, look us up on the web at http://www.CaliforniaCivilLiberties.org/.

You can also find us on Facebook at
https://www.facebook.com/californiacivilliberties.

Or look us up on Twitter at https://twitter.com/CalCivilLiberty